Yes She Came

A black woman's journey through luv & lust

Clarisse LIBENE

Yes She Came

A black woman's journey through luv & lust

From the same author :
Healthy Hair Healthy Me
Kids Hair Academy

Copyright @2018 Clarisse LIBENE
Editing : Clarisse LIBENE
Cover : La Beauté Digitale
Photography : Jessica Felicio

www.clarisselibene.fr

Content

Acknowledgements

I want to thank my family members, my sister, my mother, my brother and my father, my godmother, my aunts, my cousins and sisters, my best friends for their unwavering support since day 1.

To my children, Ruben & Serena who will maybe read these lines one day and discover another side of their mother's personality.

To you my readers who have been, with your comments, letters, emails and your presence a support without even realizing it.

For you, with you, thanks to you.

orgasm

/ˈɔːgaz(ə)m/

noun

the climax of sexual excitement, characterized by intensely pleasurable feelings centred in the genitals and (in men) experienced as an accompaniment to ejaculation.

verb

have an orgasm.

Synonym

climax, come.

Foreword

Sex is such a taboo subject within the African Diaspora. Whether you are a Black woman based in Dakar, Paris, Dallas or Kingston, it is hard for us women to talk openly about our sexuality. Seen, perceived and used as sexual objects for centuries, we have been denied the right to cum. To receive orgasms. To be pleased. To be loved.

Yes She Came is here is to provide you with a new way to see your sexuality and sensuality. To trigger parts of you you've been denying. To launch a conversation with your friends, family members, your man maybe, but most importantly with yourself. To change this internal dialog, that song you keep repeating over and over again. That song that says you are not enough or perhaps too much. That you you do not deserve to live the sexual life you aspire to have. Because GOOD sex is an essential part of life, a sacred act, moment, that we all have the right to live.

From Anjou with Love

Clarisse

Part 1 : The journey

The black woman

Strong yet so vulnerable
The black woman
Love her, spoil her
Respect her
She deserves your warm arms
To remember she is not alone
To conquer this world
Celebrate her
She is offering her best
Her heart
Her opened chest
The black woman

Dear Brother

Dear   brother
If   only   you   knew
How   much   we   love   you

And   we   are   here,   brother
Trying   to   understand
What   happened   to   you
What   happened   to   us
To   our   love,   our   sacred   connection
To   our   common   power,   our   blessed   union

Oh   !   Brother   !
If   only   you   knew
All   the   energy   we   put   in   loving   you
Despite   the   eyes   of   these   other   men
Trying   to   catch   a   breath   of   our   essence
That   is   forever   dedicated   to   you

Despite   our   loneliness
And   sometimes,   your   lack   of   tenderness
Oh   !   Brother   !
If   only   you   knew
How much we need you

In that train

I remember the 1st time we met
Like it was yesterday
We were sitting in that train
And your eyes,
Kept staring at me
I was hypnotized

At first it felt uncomfortable
The second day I raised my head and noticed your lips
Daydreaming then
Of our first kiss

The third day
You came in my way
I noticed your hands
Imagining them on my breast
Feeling your breath on my neck

The fourth day
May be a monday
I could not focus anymore
My mind was somewhere else
I was already feeling you opening my legs

The fifth time we saw each other,
You had your elbows on your knees
Your face in your hands

Staring at me
Defying me

Who would be the first
To bob down
Who would be the first
To lower the guards
Who would be the first
To stand up and talk
Who would be the first
To drop a number and walk

It was only a matter of seconds
Before I turned my head down
A matter of minutes
Before I smiled
A matter of hours
Before our first talk
A matter of days
Before we made love

Distance

She could stare at him for hours
These lines
These curves
Untouchable
Such a curse
Guess she will have
Instead
To take care
Of hers

Black

He didn't have to say a word
I knew from his eyes what he wanted
The thoughts that came to his mind when he saw me
Crossing my legs at the table of this café
Black I said to the waiter
That's how I like it most I continued
He was listening
Reading my lips
No milk no sugar no cream
He smiled, I laughed
I will come tonite
I said to myself
I will come with him.

Rising

He was intimidated.
He could not put his hands on me.
But I looked down on his pants.
I knew it.
He was as horny as I was.
Wet as I was.

I wanted him to glide through me.
Now.
It that elevator.
But I had to make him wait.
He could not say a word.
He was breathing.
Deep.
I was inhaling his smell.
Quick.
In that elevator.

Hot chocolate

Come take a sip
Of my hot chocolate
This pure nectar
That comes from my thighs
Touch it, suck this foam
That comes out when I wine
Lick it, make me moan
And reach the divine

A certain T.

You know I'm not asking for much
I am just full of love for you
You know I'm not asking for much
I will never again leave you
I know it is hard to trust
I know you are scared
But if we only focus on the worst
We will just keep being afraid

And miss the opportunity
To have you inside of me
Our hands connected
When you penetrate me
To moan together
Make our sounds last for an eternity

This love I have for you
This connection that we have
Intellectual, spiritual
Has the power to transform you
To elevate you and reveal you
It worked on me already
I just want to share it with you
My love

I know you saw my power
Even before I realized who I was
Reason why I am not asking for much

You already gave so much, shared so much,
Did so much, loved so much

I know you are afraid
Of not being enough
Of me destroying you
Hurting your feelings, your masculine
Your essence, Your divine

My angel, be reassured
My love is only love
My nectar is pure love
My energy is pure love
Yours only
Eternally

Accepting

The most difficult challenge,
I have ever had to face.
No escape, I have to accept.
My love. Unconditional.
Your friendship. Undeniable.
My feelings. Uncontrollable.

Accepting.
To create something new.
Explore new territories.
To leave my comfort zone.
Build new memories

Knowing that this new way
We are trying to find
This new path
We are so afraid to follow
May separate us
Bring the worst of us
Lead us to words we might regret
Texts, talks and conversations, we wish we would forget.

The right distance. The right time.
The right tone. The right smile.

Letting go of the old.
Embracing the new.

Enjoy the can's
Forget the could's

Of this journal, I hold so tight.
Of my love, I stop trying to fight.

Accepting.
I love you.
Letting go.
I can't control you.

Let it go

Surrender
Let it go
Let the old go and give space for the new
Stop repeating that old story over and over again
I was this, I was that
He did this, He did that
They did this, They did that
Let it go and trust
Stop looking for the miracle outside
Look at the mirror and admire
It's right here, in front of you
It's always been there, it's you
For whom it may concern

Unapologetic

That day she decided that in bed or elsewhere she would become her true self.
And yes she came!

One summer

One summer, a month, of freedom, of being myself, of finding myself.
Meeting, talking, sharing, fucking, coming, smiling, screaming, mourning, forgetting, dreaming.
Reading, writing, drinking, believing, swimming, fantasizing, breathing, masturbating, loving, fucking, living, drunk, sunk.
One Stop, contemplating, One talk, meditation. One prayer, appreciation.
Dancing, breathing, laughing, licking, sucking, inhaling, voodooing Kissing, Sweating, Swallowing, eating, savoring, consuming, devouring.
Waiting each other, hearing. Listening to each other, spilling.
Staring at one another, smiling. Loving each other, coming.
One Summer

Hard to find

45 min of play
She was wet ready
He must be too
She knew, she thought, she was sure
He was 40, after all, not a boy

She put her hand down there and... nothing
To grab
The stick was flat
Like a heavy used tire
About to retire

Is it her? What didn't she do?
It has nothing to do with you
A little voice said in her head
His poor diet, excessive worry instead

She had to recognize
He couldn't get his thing up
So she started to suck
Slowly
Taking her time
Wisely

She heard him moan
She felt she was no longer alone
That afternoon she came
Orgasmically
She realized she gave more than her body
Her soul her love
Her creative energy
Were the things missing
To her Mr B.

Recovering

34 days
Since the last time you touched me
34 days
Since the last time you held me
I haven't recovered yet
No desire for anyone I can't get wet
You left something inside of me
A part of your doubt and insecurity
I need to recover
Becoming me

Queening

She knew she didn't have to make too many efforts.
Her eyes were enough to catch him in her web
She knew she was the queen of her realm
She only had to decide who she wanted to invite
Who she gave the right to come inside
Taste her flavour
For now or forever

The sweeter the lick

They started playing
She was wet, Ready
Waiting for him to get inside
One touch on his pants
Nothing. He is not hard. Damn. It.

The smell of her oils and perfumes were filling up the room.
Coconut oil. Her best ally
Rubbed in her hands
Poured on his back

Her moaning was not enough
Her dancing was not enough.
She needed to go down
Give him head to wake him up
Make it stand hard and strong so he could glide through her warmth.

She did, what she considered her job
Methodically
Sucking holding pressing caressing

The sweater the lick. The harder the stick
He was ready
She smiled. He moaned .
May I get you inside of me now?

She didn't wait for the answer.

She was in charge. She had control .
And that afternoon, She came

What is wrong with me?

I don't know what is wrong with me
When I am alone
I cum so easily
But as soon as he is with me
Orgasm seems to become a fantasy
A dream that will never become reality
Something must be wrong about me
How come I can please myself alone
And he never seems to please me
Does he really love me?
Or is he trying to perform a show
Pleasing his ego
Forgetting making love
Is not something done in solo
What is wrong with me ?
Maybe I should talk to him
But how is he gonna receive
This news that says so much about us?
About our love, our lost chemistry
Oh ... what is wrong with me?

Love was the answer

Almost a year later
A year after they first met
A year after they tried
And she realized he was not ready

He sends a text
Asking if she was still mad
"Never been never will" she answered
"Why would I?"
"I just, don't think you got what it takes to be in a relationship. .. with me..." she added .
"What does it take?" He replied... just for his education he added.

She thought about it for a minute
What did it take to be in a relationship with her?

Four letters crossed her soul
One word that symbolizes it all:
"Love" was her answer

How do you want to be loved?

How do you need to be loved?
She realized she was not able to answer this question yet even though she had been in different relationship. Some shorter than her 15 years marriage.
She sat down and wrote
"
I need him to tell me I am beautiful
I need him to protect me physically touch me hold me
I need him to spend his quality time with me
"
This time she didn't want to let frustration dictate the way she would communicate him her core desires.
This time she decided she would teach him how to love her because she knew she deserved it.

Begging

You have no right
To look at me like that
You have no right
To trigger this inside of me
Each time I cross your eyes
I was raised to keep my head high
Not to open my legs on first request
You have no right
To make me think I am weak
Not the goddess I was educated to become
You had no right
But I am giving it to you now
Take your power Black man
Give it to me
Penetrate me
You have no right
To do this to me
Unless I beg you
To come inside of me
Would you do this for me?

It's been a while

They had not seen each other
For more than 10 years
Her belly got thicker
She was not at ease

Room 765, she told him
Sure she gave him the information already
One hour later , he entered the room
There she was, on this bed, horny

She could not believe she was there
In front of the first men who came inside her
She was ready to offer herself again
More than 10 years later

All this time, she had been waiting for this moment
Where he would glide his hands in her sacred
Kiss her, tell her how beautiful she is
Lick her, tell her how tasty she still is

She did not want to make any move
She was excited, yes, but she wanted him to be in charge
To make love to her, comfort her, reassure her,
With his magic finger, his magic tongue, his magic cock
She knew he had this power

When he went down on her
So slowly her all body started shivering
She held her breath first, then deeply breathed
Her mind was in the clouds, she was meditating

He started licking, the peak of her clit
Sucking her, before a second lick
Stronger, then a bit faster
Baby please don't stop,
Make it last forever

She wanted to return the favor
And take his cock in her mouth
While he was licking her
She just could not, focus on both
Giving him pleasure and take her own

He did not ask for anything though
Taking very seriously his mission
His assignment for the day
Make her cum papy,
Her man doesn't know how to play

Her nectar was becoming lighter
Her cream turned into juice
It was time to invade her
She was so tight, it was so smooth

Her delicate moaning
Her shy and sweet voice
Turned into heavy screaming

The dragon was unleashed
The fire was burning

I want to feel you deep
Inside of me honey
He stopped for a moment
Kissed her and executed her prayer

She could feel all his strength inside her
His weight on top of her
His sweat flowing on her skin
His power getting bigger from within

His moaning came from the depths of his soul
He wanted to please her so much, that he lost all control
He hit so hard inside of her, she could not keep it
She asked him to go faster though, her hands on her clit

Her waist beads were magnetic
Their sounds were hypnotic
The music they were doing together
The beats, the sounds, stayed in their minds forever

She felt her womb contracting
She couldn't take anymore of him
Her legs were shaking
Her breath, shorter, non existing

Her orgasm was deep
True expression of her love for him
So true she did not feel him cum inside her

Without notice, simultaneously, they came together

Love is a decision

She is there, this magazine staring at her.
She takes it, unconvinced she would learn anything. She goes
through some pages.
Horoscope, Leo page

They said sex was her drive in life
The way she expressed herself and her creativity
They said the planets would send her 2 types of men
One who would be there for her in all domains except in the
bedroom
The other would provide her everything she needs in bed but
nowhere else.
The planets, they said, would force her to question herself on the link
between love and sex.

A year went by and there she is
The planets didn't lie.
Mr. T, Mr. I.

Both there for her, at a different level
Physical for one, for the other, spiritual.

She kicked both out of her life though
She wants it all, She needed both
Could she have both?
Why would one come without the other?
She was all of this
Love was all of this

She could not divide herself,
Being loved a way, and not the other
It had no meaning,
It had no flavor.

Then a thought came to her mind
Spirit was talking to her
Love is a decision, darling
You should know better

And that day
She made a commitment
To herself, to her heart, to her love
She realized she did not need
Anybody to complete her
She was already whole
The love she's been seeking
Was lying there
Inside her soul

Interlude

4 Love is patient, love is kind. It does not envy, it does not boast, it is not proud. 5 It does not dishonor others, it is not self-seeking, it is not easily angered, it keeps no record of wrongs. 6 Love does not delight in evil but rejoices with the truth. 7 It always protects, always trusts, always hopes, always perseveres.

8 Love never fails. But where there are prophecies, they will cease; where there are tongues, they will be stilled; where there is knowledge, it will pass away. 9 For we know in part and we prophesy in part, 10 but when completeness comes, what is in part disappears. 11 When I was a child, I talked like a child, I thought like a child, I reasoned like a child. When I became a man, I put the ways of childhood behind me. 12 For now we see only a reflection as in a mirror; then we shall see face to face. Now I know in part; then I shall know fully, even as I am fully known.

13 And now these three remain: faith, hope and love. But the greatest of these is love.
1 Corinthians 13

I could not imagine finishing this book without the part 2 you are about to read. Because this journey, through luv & lust, was inspired by my own life, but also the ones of the women who share their stories and experiences with me since 2008.

As you know I've been married for almost 15 years and as you may also know, I am in a non committed relationship now. Sex is a very important subject for me and should be for everyone, whether you are single or married. It is the center of all creation. It is sacred. It is making love.
I have always asked myself questions regarding sexuality and being raised by a senegalese mother was a blessing in that matter. Solutions came naturally to me : in Senegal, selfcare rituals are part of our DNA.
Nonetheless, ending a 15 years old relationship is not easy, and I have had to rediscover myself, asking myself what I loved about sex, how I want to make love, be in love, and be loved.

Deconstructing habits to create new ones that would be at my own image, according to my values and principles. Not as a couple, but as me. Separate what had been intertwined for years, and sometimes, at the expense of my own pleasure, femininity, and self confidence.

In my journey as a life coach, I have realised that most of my clients had difficulties living the sexlife they wanted, I thought that sharing my own journey would be beneficial.
I also know where you come from, sister, and understand that it is not easy for you, for us, to see a therapist and talk openly and frankly about sexuality and relationships.

Because of our history, from slavery to colonialism, our bodies and our sexuality have been everybody else's but ours. I sincerely think that lead us to a certain level of ignorance towards our desires. We do not know how we want to be loved. We were never given the right to express things for ourselves.

The second reason why this part two was important for me is because we are struggling to get men. This is an epidemic that is hitting us globally. Not having *any* man. But having a long committed relationship. A man we can rise with and lean upon.

Black women are struggling everywhere and to me, there is something very spiritual about this. Why would it be so difficult for a whole generation of black women all over the globe, who are educated, smart, beautiful to have the relationships they want? Where are our men? What is going on? In humble opinion, this has to do with an introspective work that needs to be done and most of all, with healing. I hope this part two will give you some tools to understand what are the forces involved, forces that are way higher than us and urge us to heal and use our creative power for ourselves, *at last*.

The second part of this book are letters addressed to you my sisters. At the end of each letter, you will be asked a question, or a series of exercises to do. I encourage you to buy yourself a journal and do the assignments written down on it. Writing is also part of the healing process. Do not undermine the power of your own words, mind and handwriting. You are a vessel for Spirit too sister, everybody knows it but us. Use your power now, and become the new you.

Part 2 : Letters to my sisters

Fear

"It is not death that a man should fear, but he should fear never beginning   to   live"
Marcus Aurelius

Hope you are doing good today and this letter finds you well. As you know, divorce has been quite a journey for me and now, after 4 years, I still thank God for letting me free. It has not been an easy path. I have been in an abuse relationship for 14 years. Why Abusive? because it was lead by fear, the perfect opposite   to   love.
Fear   of   not   being   enough   to   find   another   man
Fear of the words he could pronounce that would again reduce my self esteem (you are fat, who do you think you are...)
Fear   my   parents   would   judge
Fear   of   disappointing   my   son   and   break   his   heart
It took me to become pregnant of my second child, and to be so anxious of announcing the news to him to realize fear was leading me   in   this   relationship.
Like many women, my children's protection gave me the power to overcome fear and decide to live. Stop surviving. But Living. Really.
And you sis, are you living?

No regrets

"Regret is a form of punishment itself"
Nouman Ali Khan

How   is   it   going   today?
Did   you   think   about   your   ex   since   this   morning?
I am sure you did. Maybe you are still thinking about the last time
you and him had sex. I am saying having sex and not making love
purposely. Making love and having sex are two different things.
We   usually   learn   it   the   hard   way.

With the multiplication of dating apps, the simple access to birth
control and this society of instant pleasure and gratification, we
have a tendency to forget that more than just a few minutes of
fun, sexual intercourse is a very powerful tool to share energy.
There are many reasons why we can have regrets after sex.
Today,   we   will   learn   why   and   how   to   recover.

There are many reasons why we can have regrets after sex :
- it was simply not good
- you did not share a real connection with our partner
- you did not really feel the desire but could not stand up
  and say no
- we realize then that we do not really know this person
- we realize that some of our needs are still not being met.
  Often, our need for intimacy and connection can be high
  and the man's attitude during intercourse can leave us
  completely empty. Did he take care of you? Did he get
  down on you? Did he try to satisfy you or was he here

looking for performance? Take but not give? Did he try to please you?
- We do not know what to do right after the intercourse (should I stay, go out of the room full of shame, can I invite him to stay, why does he leave?)
- The person was not in a positive state of mind.

I really would like to focus on this last point because many women do not realize how powerful men's sperm can be. The sperm of men is actually the purest representation of their state of mind. You literally absorb their energy during sex. Sex is never meaningless, with or without a condom. The simple act of ejaculation is an energetic discharge. When he is angry, you become more angry. When he feels helpless, you feel more helpless, when he feels empty, you will feel more empty, while reloading   him.

If this happens to you, here are my recommendations

First,   detox

- Pour a bath, with warm water, add a sprig of sage and hibiscus leaves + 3 drops of essential oils of cinnamon, tea tree, lavender or lemongrass.
- Meditate in the water and focus on your breathing. Whatever negative feelings you have been coming, imagine that they are leaving your body. Feel the emotion go away.
- Repeat this bath every morning or every evening for 40 days. And after each bath, if you feel the need, take your diary and note what comes to mind at that time. End with

a prayer asking God to help you restore your mind, body, and soul. Continue the rest of your activities as usual.

- Rest for a while and try not to have sex in the next 40 days. If you are married or engaged, try not to have sex with your man for the next 40 days. You must heal.
- After this period of deep cleansing and refocusing, you will be ready to move on to the second phase of your healing process, introspection and meditation.

Second, introspection

I invite you to ask yourself the following questions. Take an afternoon to answer. The 40 days of abstinence should help you reconnect with the feelings you had during your last sexual encounter. If you want to cry, let it be and cry. If you want to scream, let it be and scream. Do not try to rationalize and analyze things in your brain but in your heart. You will be surprised to see how much your body and your heart have things to say to you.

- Why did you have sex with this person? What need did you want to satisfy? Did you want to feel protected? Loved? Respected? Admired? Connected?

- What was the nature of your discussions before sexual intercourse? What did this person look like to you? What adjectives would you use to describe his state of mind?
- If you could choose a color to represent his state of mind, what would it be?

If you could choose a color to represent his sperm, what would that color be?
- How did you feel during sex? Close your eyes and try to remember that moment. To dive deeper into this emotion. What did he look like? (Often, you will not remember the person but an archetype, an animal...). Describe it.
- How did you feel when he touched you before sex during and   after?

These questions are here to help you understand what are the needs that are not yet met, what are you looking for in a relationship, what was the energy with which you were charged during sex and what were the signals that your body sent you.

So angry

"You have the right to be mad"
Solange Knowles

Divorce or separation is often compared to bereavement. With its phases, more or less long, that we recognize more or less.

Anger management is tough. Especially for us, black women. Because we are afraid to be considered the Angry Black woman, we are afraid to express our anger. To scream. To say no. We keep this anger inside our belly, or even inside our womb, generating all types of disorders from gastric pain, ulcer, to fibroids. Anger, kept in our bodies, and transmitted from generations to generations. Until we heal.

But to heal, we have to let this anger go. We have to let in burn, before it burns us from the inside out.

I have developed a series of exercises that worked for myself, my son and my clients over the years. It includes the four elements, fire, water, earth and air. Are you mad at your ex sis? Do you surprise yourself insulting him in your head when you are alone? Do you feel like punching him in the face each time you want to see him or hear his voice. If so, try this first part of the exercise.

- Take one hour or two to do this exercise. Make sure you are alone with no distraction. Switch off your phone and go to your room. Light the candle of your choice. Go to your bed and sit. Or in any space in your house where you feel comfortable.
- Take a piece of white paper and a black pen. Write all of the Insults you want to tell him. Freely. If you want to scream, scream. if you want to cry, cry. Write everything down, until you no longer have anything to say. Until you feel exhausted and tired.
- Now that this is done, go to your kitchen. Take a bowl that can resist fire. Take the paper and burn it. Put it in the bowl. Watch the flames consume your anger.
- Blow on the embers until they are turned into ashes.
- Add water to the ashes to end the fire completely
- Take the ashes and bury them in the plant of your choice in your house. This anger will turn into life, just like it will inside of you.

With this first exercise, you should already feel better. The exercise is not over. For this anger to be gone for a long period of time, you need to do it each time you feel anger burning you.

When money is involved

"But   *you*   *can't*   *use*   *my*   *phone"*
Erykah   *badu*

Erykah warned us so many years ago. Beyonce and the Destiny's child did the same. TLC were so clear in their message. And yet, here we are, with this asshole using us and our money.

- You put all of your money on the table and you realise he's been saving for years.
He asked you to cut all expenses in two equal parts.
You are here struggling with the kids when he can enjoy holidays alone.

Sis', let me tell you one thing, you are not alone. I can not tell you how many of my clients have been facing divorce and break ups over the past 5 years. With the same pattern, he was ready, you were not. You feel guilty, stupid. You never should have accepted this. You never should have entered this game. Don't blame yourself. This experience happened for a reason. You may don't know it yet, but soon, you will.

Forgetting   him

"Body is memory"
Sadh Guru

In many spiritualities, Indian or African, body and mind are one. When we get married, we attach two bodies, two spirits and two families. This link becomes even stronger when you have children. See the roots of a tree that intermingle under the earth to form this new family unit, this new life that emerges. Moreover, when one says of a woman that she has cast a spell on a man so that he does not deceive her or stay with her, it is said that she has tied him up. *Here again, the importance of words.*

Understand that to recover from a divorce or a breakup, doing an emotional or psychological work is not enough. This work must also have its physical materialization, at each step that we go through.

The body is memory. Have you ever felt the smell of your ex-companion in his absence, are you still sometimes feeling the presence of his hand in yours when you walk in the street? Do you go to bed feeling very cold. His body missing in your bed? To have a strong pain in the lower belly, as if your uterus was torn to pieces.
This phenomenon is well known to people who have undergone amputation. It's called the ghost member syndrome. Pain, more or less intense, felt exactly where the missing limb was sitting.

For SadhGuru, the physical body is only memory. And it is

because our body is "polluted" by a memory that no longer belongs to it that it resists change, that it refuses the separation. In one of his lectures he says this eloquent phrase "An eye that is charged with memory can not see things as they are".

When separating two bodies that were one, it is normal that you feel the absence of this other body, omnipresent previously, around you and in you. If the physical body is absent, the etheric body, aura, or energy of your ex, will take longer to leave you. Your body is charged with the memory of this other. Your senses have been charged with the memory of each other's body. To divorce or to break up is to renounce to this other, his body, his smell, his warmth, his skin. If your mind wants to forget, your whole body refuses to free itself from this memory. It is a comfort zone. A protective cocoon the body does not want to leave.

Accepting

To heal is accepting things as they are.
To heal and let go is recognizing the good and the bad, your part of responsibility, your sadness, your emptiness. It is also realizing that you will never forget. Him. That he was there for a reason. The moment you know the why and connect the dots, the better you feel.

To accept separation is to deal with this memory that is no longer yours and keep it at the right place. To be able to turn it on when you want to. To be able to switch it off when it no longer serves you.

To accept separation is to make sure those memories do not jeopardize your present life and your capacity to move forward.

And to allow yourself to discover you, as a unique human being. Complete, with all your shades and facettes. Becoming you again. I wish you good luck in this journey sis. I wish love, and lust, if you wish ;-)

Your sister who loves you deeply,
Clarisse

Printed in Great Britain
by Amazon